For our loving dog, Ghost, who thinks all bouncing spheres belong to him.

Para nuestro querido perro, Ghost, que cree que todas las esferas que rebotan le pertenecen.

—E.E.

To the love of my life, thank you for making me smile every single day.

Al amor de mi vida, gracias por hacerme sonreír todos los días.

—A.L.

Spheres All Year / Esferas todo el año
Paperback first edition • June 2023 • ISBN: 978-1-958629-23-9
Board Book first edition • June 2023 • ISBN: 978-1-958629-17-8
eBook first edition • June 2023 • ISBN: 978-1-958629-20-8

Written by Elizabeth Everett, Text © 2023
Illustrated by Anuki López, Illustrations © 2023

Project Manager, Cover and Book Design: Caitlin Burnham
Transadaptation by: Andrea Batista
Spanish-language Consultant: Ali Trujillo
Editors: Marlee Brooks and Hannah Thelen
Editorial Assistants: Liliann Albelbaisi, Emilee Rae Hibshman, and Chloe Cattaneo

Available in English as Spheres All Year
Hardcover first edition • June 2023 • ISBN: 978-1-958629-22-2
Paperback first edition • June 2023 • ISBN: 978-1-958629-21-5
eBook first edition • June 2023 • ISBN: 978-1-958629-18-5

Teacher's Guide available at the Educational Resources page of ScienceNaturally.com.

Published by:
    Science, Naturally! – An imprint of Platypus Media, LLC
    750 First Street NE, Suite 700
    Washington, DC 20002
    202-465-4798 • Fax: 202-558-2132
    Info@ScienceNaturally.com • ScienceNaturally.com

Distributed to the book trade by:
    National Book Network (North America)
        301-459-3366 • Toll-free: 800-462-6420
        CustomerCare@NBNbooks.com • NBNbooks.com
    NBN International (worldwide)
        NBNi.Cservs@IngramContent.com • Distribution.NBNi.co.uk

Library of Congress Control Number: 2022948137

10 9 8 7 6 5 4 3 2 1

SPHERES ALL YEAR

ESFERAS TODO EL AÑO

Written by Elizabeth Everett

Illustrated by Anuki López

Science, Naturally!
An imprint of Platypus Media, LLC
Washington, D.C.

Spheres are round just like a ball—
they have no points or corners at all.

Las esferas son redondas como un balón,
sin puntas y sin esquinas en ninguna dirección.

Not flat like a circle, a sphere you can hold.
Across the ground, they can be rolled.

No son como un círculo, que es plano.
A las esferas las puedes llevar en tu mano.

To make a sphere, three dimensions unite:
these 3-D objects have length, width, and height.

sphere / esfera

radius / radio

pyramid / pirámide

height / altura

base / base

rectangle / rectangulo

height / altura

width / ancho

length / longitud

Para hacer una esfera, tres dimensiones se unen con exactitud.
Son cuerpos tridimensionales con altura, ancho y longitud.

Look all around you and it will be clear,
there are so many different kinds of spheres!

*Mira a tu alrededor y lo verás claro,
¡hay esferas por todos lados!*

**Summer, fall, winter, and spring:
discover the spheres each season will bring!**

*Verano, otoño, invierno y primavera:
¡en cada estación descubrirás esferas!*

Big scoops of ice cream taste just right,
cooling us off in the warm sunlight.

*Bolas de helado con el mejor sabor
nos refrescan dulcemente en el calor.*

Turtle eggs hatch in their underground nest.
The moon will guide them, there's no time to rest!

Huevos de tortuga empiezan a romper.
La luna los guiará, ¡no hay tiempo que perder!

Sweet round cherries with hard pits inside
leave all of our fingertips purple-dyed.

*Cerezas dulces y redondas con semillas duras en su interior
nos pintan los dedos morados y hasta mi cara tiene color.*

A brightly colored beach ball tossed in the air
makes a hot day something special to share.

En la playa, una pelota colorida por el aire vuela.
Es un día caluroso y no tenemos que ir a la escuela.

A soccer ball rolls through freshly cut grass.
The players kick it and shout, "Here, pass!"

Un balón de fútbol rueda por el césped recién cortado.
Los jugadores la patean y gritan "¡Pásala para este lado!".

Soon orange pumpkins grow all around,
and bright red leaves crunch on the ground.

Calabazas anaranjadas crecen por todos lados,
y las hojas rojas crujen en el suelo dorado.

Warm sugared donuts make quite a snack
after jumping in leaves and raking them back.

Donas calientes y azucaradas son un buen bocadillo.
Saltamos sobre las hojas y las juntamos con el rastrillo.

Eating candy as the air gets chilly,
the costumes we see are all so silly!

Comemos dulces cuando empieza a hacer frío.
¡Los disfraces que vemos son todos tan divertidos!

Walking outside, cold snow starts to fall.
It's time for a hat with a pom-pom ball.

Salimos a caminar, la nieve empieza a caer.
Mi gorro con un pompón ya me tengo que poner.

A set of three snowballs, carefully packed,
makes a snow friend, haphazardly stacked.

Tres bolas de nieve, armadas cuidadosamente,
hacen un amigo de nieve que se sostiene con mucha suerte.

To finish the year, we roll cookie dough.
We try to be patient, but the oven's so slow!

A fin de año, hacer bollos de masa de galleta es un encanto.
Intentamos ser pacientes, ¡pero el horno tarda tanto!

Outside the window, the full moon is bright
on a long and peaceful starlit night.

Brilla la luna llena, que miro por mi ventana.
Es una muy tranquila noche; descanso hasta la mañana.

The weather warms, green colors abound.
The Sun comes out, shining and round.

Con el clima cálido, el color verde vuelve.
El redondo Sol sale y su luz todo lo envuelve.

A little seed that we plant in the earth
becomes a red radish popping out of the dirt.

Una semillita que plantamos en la tierra
se convierte en un rábano rojo que sale entre la hierba.

Purple flower puffs line the street,
making the air smell fresh and sweet.

Flores moradas se alinean en la acera.
El dulce y fresco aire nos dice que es primavera.

Watch sparkling bubbles float away—
what a wonderful way to spend the day!

Mira cómo flotan las burbujas en el aire.
¡Qué manera tan maravillosa de pasar la tarde!

You've discovered the spheres each season brings,
from summer and fall to winter and spring.

*Has descubierto que cada estación trae consigo esferas,
desde el verano y el otoño hasta el invierno y la primavera.*

**And don't forget that Earth is a sphere,
where we spend each day, all year!**

*La Tierra es también una esfera, aunque esto parezca extraño,
¡donde pasamos cada hora, cada día y todo el año!*

Spheres can be as big as the stars that twinkle,
or as teeny tiny as a rainbow sprinkle.

Tan grandes como una estrella pueden ser las esferas,
o tan pequeñas como las perlas de azúcar que saboreas.

Look around you and it will be clear,
there are so many different kinds of spheres!

Mira a tu alrededor y lo verás claro,
¡hay esferas por todos lados!

What Are 2-D Shapes?
¿Qué son las figuras bidimensionales?

Dimensions are used to measure and describe shapes. They can tell us how long a shape is, how wide, and how high.

Some shapes only have two dimensions, like length and width <u>or</u> height and width. These are called 2-D shapes.

When a shape is 2-D, it is flat. Examples of 2-D shapes include circles, squares, and triangles.

Las dimensiones se utilizan para medir y describir figuras. Ellas nos pueden decir cuánto mide una figura de largo, de ancho o de alto.

Algunas figuras sólo tienen dos dimensiones, como largo (o longitud) y ancho <u>o</u> largo y altura. Estas figuras se llaman figuras bidimensionales.

Cuando una figura es bidimensional, es plana. Ejemplos de figuras bidimensionales son los círculos, los cuadrados y los triángulos.

What Are 3-D Shapes?

¿Qué son las figuras tridimensionales?

Some shapes have three dimensions, like length, width, <u>and</u> height. These are called 3-D shapes.

Unlike 2-D shapes, 3-D shapes are never flat. Examples of 3-D shapes include spheres, cubes, and pyramids.

Algunas figuras tienen tres dimensiones, como largo (o longitud), ancho y altura. Estas se llaman figuras tridimensionales.

A diferencia de las figuras bidimensionales, las figuras tridimensionales nunca son planas. Ejemplos de figuras tridimensionales son las esferas, los cubos y las pirámides.

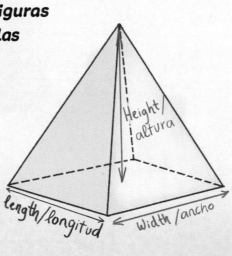

Meet the Author and Illustrator

Elizabeth Everett spent 16 years as a classroom teacher before venturing into writing. She is inspired by her energetic youngster, Jalen, and his love for books. She currently lives in Colorado with her family where they love spending time outdoors in the Western sun. She is the author of *This Is the Sun* and *Twinkle, Twinkle, Daytime Star*. She can be reached at Elizabeth.Everett@ScienceNaturally.com.

Anuki López studied Fine Arts at the University of Seville in Spain. She has been drawing since she can remember; a notebook and colored pencils were her favorite toys. She loves working and living her life as an illustrator, bringing children illustrations that are full of color, magic, humor, animals, respect, and, of course, love. You can see more of her art on her Instagram page, @anukilopez.